Three Minutes
for the Soul

Series Preface

The volumes in NCP's "7 x 4" series offer a meditation a day for four weeks, a bite of food for thought, a reflection that lets a reader ponder the spiritual significance of each and every day. Small enough to slip into a purse or coat pocket, these books fit easily into everyday routines.

Three Minutes for the Soul

Reflections to Start the Day

Gerhard Bauer

Foreword by
Marc Foley

New City Press
Hyde Park, New York

Published in the United States by New City Press
202 Cardinal Rd., Hyde Park, NY 12538
www.newcitypress.com
©2007 New City Press (English translation)

Translated by Edward Hagmann from the original German edition
Drei Minuten für die Seele
©2006 Neue Stadt, Munich, Germany

Cover design by Durva Correia

Library of Congress Cataloging-in-Publication Data:

Bauer, Gerhard, Dr.
  [Drei Minuten für die Seele. English]
  Three minutes for the soul : reflections to start the day / Gerhard Bauer ;
foreword by Marc Foley.
       p. cm. -- (4 x 7)
  Includes bibliographical references and index.
  ISBN 978-1-56548-275-3 (alk. paper)
  1. Meditations.   2. Christian life--Catholic authors.   I. Title.
BX2182.3.B38 2007
242' .2--dc22   2007022317

Printed in the United States of America

Contents

Foreword 7

one
Good Morning Dear Self

1. A Look in the Mirror 10
2. Treat Yourself 12
3. Praising the Day
   Before the Evening 14
4. Evening Habits 16
5. My Way 18
6. The Singing Bowl 20
7. Attentiveness 22

two
The Mystery of the Present Moment

1. (No) Child's Play 26
2. As If It Were the Last Day 28
3. Stress-Free in a Minute 30
4. Just for Today 32
5. I Haven't Time 34
6. A Day of Awareness 35
7. Breaks 37

three
I Love and Do What You Will

1. Love and Do What You Will..40
2. Take the Bull by the Horns.......................................42
3. What Remains...44
4. The Golden Rule..46
5. Advance Preparation...48
6. Do You Know
   What Hurts Me?..50
7. Called by Name...52

four
Seeking Good

1. A Resounding Yes 56
2. The Carpet..58
3. Within Ourselves or Nowhere..................................60
4. The Whole in a Fragment 62
5. Seeking and Finding God in All Things 64
6. God Is Always Other..66
7. Everything Begins with Desire..............................68

Foreword

Anchored in Eternity

In his book *The Saturated Self,* psychologist Kenneth Gergen argues that the massive increase of social stimulation that we are exposed to in our society is reaching saturation point. We do not need to read Gergen's book to know the truth of his assertion; we have only to consult our shattered nerves for verification. All day long, our over-stimulated society bombards us with a barrage of information, through newspapers, billboards, radio, television, Internet or fax. Furthermore, we have lost the predictability of privacy; cell-phones and e-mail have made us completely accessible to others, and everyone expects an instant reply. How often have we said to ourselves, "I don't even have time to think!" Or "If I only had a quiet moment with myself." The truth is, we actually do have quiet moments during the day, because the clamor of our minds drowns out the Eternal Silence dwelling within our hearts. Because we live at breakneck speed, it is unrealistic to expect our minds to come to a halt the moment we lay down our work. In fact, in our quiet moments it seems as if the noise of our minds increases; every fear, future project, and scrap of unfinished business comes rushing in and clamors for our attention. What we need are mental moorings — a word, an idea or an image that will anchor our minds and prevent them from being caught up in a whirlwind of emotion.

Dr. Gerhard Bauer, former spiritual director of the Augsburg seminary, provides us with such mental anchors in the present book. His reflections are brief and to the point. Each contains a single thought, a simple mental mooring upon which our minds can fasten amidst the storms of daily life. We live and work in time, but God has planted "the timeless into our hearts" (Eccl 3:11). Bauer's reflections keep our minds anchored in the Timeless One.

Marc Foley, O.C.D.

Good Morning Dear Self

one

1 A Look in the Mirror

When we look at ourselves in the mirror during our daily morning ablutions, what thoughts go through our mind? Maybe we're still too tired to take a really close look at ourselves, not to mention consciously accepting the face that looks back at us. Yet, that's what we're supposed to do. Who's supposed to like the person who doesn't like himself or herself?

But honestly, when it comes to the face in the mirror, couldn't I sometimes say: "The person I am, sadly greets the person I'd like to be"? How far I am from my ideals and goals! It's certainly good to have some for oneself, but they can deceive me into believing something false. Accepting the real image in the mirror is one of the major tasks of our life. During my morning ablutions, I have a chance to do this. If in the morning I say yes to myself, just as I am, if I don't avoid the image in the mirror, then the day is already half won.

Someone once gave me a tip that makes this easier for me: "Try some time, when you look in the mirror, to immediately find three good qualities in yourself. Then say to yourself, 'Good morning, dear self!' "

Incidentally, what's to stop me from also looking for three good qualities in those who will cross my path today?

2 Treat Yourself

"Treat yourself!" I didn't take this appeal from a psychology magazine. It comes from a great medieval saint, Bernard of Clairvaux, from the first half of the twelfth century. He is writing these words to his former pupil, then Pope Eugenius III, because he is concerned about the latter's activism. He invites him to take a break now and then from his stressful life in order to reflect: "How much longer are you going to devote your attention to everyone else, but not to yourself!"

Bernard is writing this because of his own experience of inner unrest. He too was no stranger to the conflict between inner life and external activity. Stress was obviously a constant reality. Precisely because he himself, as a monk, frequently reached the end of his rope, he was able to advise others: "Remember to treat yourself! I'm not saying do this all the time, I'm not saying do this most of the time, but do it now and then.

You are there for others; be there for yourself, too, at least after the others."

If we take these words with us, maybe our fellow human beings will also find us more bearable.

Praising the Day Before the Evening

The old saying, "One shouldn't praise the day before the evening," is true. We know perfectly well that anything can still happen today, that anything can go wrong. I'm not even guaranteed that I'll still be alive this evening.

Nevertheless, as a good friend taught me recently, for just that reason we can praise the day even before the evening; for example in the morning, upon awakening, during our morning ablutions, over breakfast or while reading these lines.

How crucial for the success of the day are those first thoughts when I wake up. Often they determine whether or not I get out of the wrong side of the bed, whether I give the new day a chance — with the pleasant and the unpleasant, the hard and the easy; with every challenge that chance can bring.

A new day lies ahead of me! That's reason enough to praise the day even before the evening.

4 Evening Habits

What were the images, feelings and thoughts we fell asleep with last night? It's worth reflecting on them again. Often there's an inner connection between our evening habits and our waking up in the morning. Did I fall asleep after a good conversation or a loving encounter, or in anger or discord? Did images and scenes of violence accompany me to the end and maybe into my dreams? Or something good that I read? Did I fall into bed from exhaustion or from having drunk too much? Or was I able, fully conscious, to surrender to a healthy sense of trust, while confidently giving the day back to the Creator?

Over the years I have grown used to quiet down, and in complete silence and with loving attention let the day pass in review, examine the images, events and feelings once more in order to really hand them over. Only then do I feel that I've really lived the day.

Then, if I'm accompanied by a good word as I fall asleep, it's already waiting for me the next morning when I wake up. As it says in the creation account in the Bible: "God saw that it was good. And there was evening and morning, a new day."

5 My Way

This morning I climbed out of bed and into my life, just as it turned out....

We often ask ourselves why our life turned out so differently from what we expected. So many possibilities and prospects seemed to attract us when we were young. We wanted to accomplish this thing and that thing. Our life was supposed to become something special, something unique!

Actually it *is* unique, however ordinary it may look. It's *my* life, on which I've left my mark. Doesn't happiness consist of sticking with my life and saying yes to it, just as it is right now?

Even if I don't always see it, I still believe there's a thread running through it. I'm confident that eventually the reason for this or that stretch, this or that detour becomes clear to me. The important thing is to continue on my way. Here the words of Werner Sprenger come to mind: "There is a path that no one walks unless you do. Paths are created as we walk them. The many paths we have not walked on are overgrown with missed opportunities. Walk your path, a path that is only created if you walk it."

6 The Singing Bowl

I'm holding in my hand a singing bowl from Tibet. Its sound is an invitation to silence and meditation. I strike it and listen to its tone slowly fade away. Silence …

Each bowl has a distinctive tone. In the same way, a friend pointed out to me, each person has his or her distinctive and unique tone, which must be made to sound. It is the personal vocation of every individual, a gift from the Creator. In order to hear God's sound in me, two things are necessary:

I need someone to strike the singing bowl and make it sound; someone to help me understand my own personal path and make it bear fruit for others.

It is good to occasionally recall the important "stimuli" in my life: a word that helped me reach a decision, an encounter in which I understood that something was right for me. Maybe also some words of encouragement: "You can do it!" Or some helpful criticism: "You could really do that differently!"

At such moments we have been, as it were, awakened from our long sleep. We sensed: "That's good, that's mine, that fits me."

A second thing is necessary: for the bowl to sound it has to be empty. To the extent that I am honest and open-minded, that I stop trying to cultivate a certain image and get over playing a long-established role, to that extent will my own sound be effective. Who wouldn't want to be fully himself or herself! Even today …

7 Attentiveness

The problem of our daily life is superficiality. We must painfully admit that often we have lost control of what happens in our life. Come evening, what do I have in my hands? The days slip like sand between my fingers, one after the other. Can that be? Can that be all?

There are experiences in which a very different note predominates, experiences that make us sit up and take notice. Alfred Delp recorded such a thoroughly shocking experience. Facing death, he wrote from the Tegel Prison, November 11, 1944:

"The world is full of God. From every pore, God rushes out to us, as it were. But we're often blind. We remain stuck in the good times and the bad times and don't experience them right up to the point where the spring flows forth from God. That's true ... for pleasant experiences as well as for unhappy ones. In everything,

God wants to celebrate encounter and asks for the prayerful response of surrender."[1]

"We're often blind." That is Alfred Delp's conclusion. Maybe it's due to the fact that our daily life often seems drab. Maybe "all" we need is a little more attentiveness! Because, according to Simone Weil, attentiveness is already tantamount to prayer, and "the peak of attentiveness touches God."

---

1. Mary Frances Coady, *With Bound Hands: A Jesuit in Nazi Germany: The Life and Selected Prison Letters of Alfred Delp* (Chicago: Loyola Press, 2003), p. 92.

The Mystery of
the Present Moment

(No)
Child's
Play

A very ordinary experience recently got me thinking, and not for the first time. I was watching some children play. They were doing so with enormous seriousness and great pleasure, as if there were nothing else and nothing more important in the world. All else was forgotten.

Once again I thought: How often do we adults, in our frantic self-importance, act as if we could capture time! At the same time we are overcome more than ever by the feeling that it's slipping between our fingers like sand. What more do we have than this moment, the present, the here and now? What would it be like if we did what we're doing right now, our task for today, with the seriousness of children who know only how to play?

The key to happiness lies in the present.

Not to be constantly in a hurry, but intent on whatever I'm doing right now, and this wholeheartedly.

2 As If It Were the Last Day

Just before falling asleep I'm startled from my nap. Thank God I was just dreaming! Dreaming about what nearly happened the day before. On the highway an oncoming car suddenly pulled out in order to pass a truck. It was heading directly toward me and it was too late to hit the brakes. I pulled to the right as far as I could, and the truck did the same. Our three vehicles just missed each other. "That was a close call!" I thought to myself. I had been lucky. For me it was like a miracle, and I thanked God for sparing my life. A prayer came to mind spontaneously: "Lord, let me always speak as if it were the last word I'm able to say. Let me always act as if it were the last act I'm to perform."

As I woke up this morning, these words were still in my head. Wouldn't they make a good leitmotif for today?

Let me always speak
as if it were the last word
I'm able to say.
Let me always act
as if it were the last act
I'm able to perform.
Let me always suffer
as if it were the last pain
I'm able to offer up.
Let me always pray
as if it were my last chance on earth
to speak with you.

(Based on a text of Chiara Lubich)

3 Stress-Free in a Minute

Who is not familiar with the daily stress that takes so much out of us and from which we often can't escape? I'm not referring to "good" stress, that zest for life that unleashes my energy, stimulates my imagination and brings joy. I'm thinking of the unhealthy stress that I often create for myself.

Unhealthy stress arises when, for example, I haven't come to terms with my present situation, when I withdraw from the here and now. I'm wandering around in the past, and then one thing or another catches up with me. Things left undone and opportunities missed surface to haunt me all the more. Or else I live in the future, dreaming or anxious about everything that could possibly happen.

Either way, the energy I need for today is sapped. Meanwhile my life is happening today! And today I can make a new start. Today, with loving attention, I can face up to the task that's now mine to do. Today — and *just* for today — I have the strength to bear the burden of my life.

I know of no other key to happiness than to say a total and fully deliberate yes to the here and now and, with love for the task each moment brings, take charge of my life. *Today* is the real thing when it comes to my life. If I take that seriously, my life becomes a little easier!

4 Just for Today

Many people still remember Pope John XXIII today, his great humanity, his goodness and joviality. His journal reveals something of the secret of his life:

"Just for today, I will try to get through the day without wanting to solve my life's problems all at once.

"Just for today, I will … not try to correct or improve others, just myself.

"Just for today I will be happy knowing that I am created for happiness.

"Just for today I will change myself to fit the circumstances, not demand that circumstances change to fit me.

"Just for today I will devote ten minutes to spiritual reading: as the body needs food so too my soul needs spiritual reading.

"Just for today, I will do a good deed and tell no one.

"Just for today I will do something for which I have no taste; I will be content with that and will try to see that no one notices.

"Just for today I will draw up an exact schedule....

"Just for today I will believe — even when circumstances seem to contradict it — that God is there for me, just as though no one else existed.

"Just for today I will not allow myself to be disheartened by the thought that I must hold out for a lifetime. I have twelve hours today for doing good."

5 I Haven't Time

"I haven't time!" How often have we hurt somebody with these words! How often have we ourselves felt let down on hearing these words from someone else! "I haven't time..." A glance at our appointment calendar confirms that almost everything is booked: the evening, the weekend, vacation time. My life? That can't possibly be!

"I haven't time for you now because I've promised somebody else I'd be there for them now." Such a statement I can understand. In any event, you can only be totally there for one person. It becomes a problem when there's never (or hardly ever) time for anything or anyone. Then we've obviously gotten lost.

Tell me who you have time for, and I'll tell you who you are. Time is among the most precious things I have to give. It can't be bought. It's a piece of me, or of my life. Let's ask ourselves: What are we taking time for today?

A Day
of
Awareness
6

One thing we can always do is make this day "a day of awareness." I owe this unusual and simple idea to a Buddhist monk from Vietnam, Thich Nhat Hanh. He advises us to devote one day of the week entirely to the practice of awareness. I've tried it and it's by no means easy. I don't need to do more or less, or anything different from what this day brings — just do everything with inner attentiveness, with full awareness, with love for the task, for the joy of living. And everything I do then, from getting up to brushing my teeth to eating breakfast, I do it all from an inner center. As I focus on always doing just this one thing and doing it totally, I'm not already thinking about rushing to the next thing. I don't leave things lying half done, I don't go on and on when I talk to the person across from me. Thus I discover the value of the present moment. In everything a serene inner composure prevails, an atmosphere of meditation. My life itself, in its ordinariness, becomes a meditation. It's really very easy, though I know how hard it is. It comes with trying. Why not today?

Breaks 7

Who hasn't felt a desire for a break from the daily routine? We want the weekend to come, a free day, vacation. Breaks are necessary. Sometimes I wonder why we don't really take advantage of the times we are "interrupted" in the course of a typical workday. Why don't we use them to gasp and catch our breath?

Our day is broken up by so many periods of waiting: in the shop or at the reception desk between clients, at the bus stop or red light, in front of the computer screen or the vending machine that won't spit out the item we want, in traffic. One minute, or maybe just a few seconds to take a deep breath, to focus on ourselves, to gather our thoughts. One of my spiritual guides called this a "prayer break." We shouldn't wear ourselves out going non-stop. We can use compulsory breaks and take a deep breath, be quiet, stop for a little while.

Maybe that's already prayer ...

Love and Do What You Will

three

Love and Do What You Will

Where would we be if everyone lived by these words of Augustine! Love makes a person blind and leads to foolishness. Where will law and order end up?

To be sure, love correctly understood, as meant by Jesus and written by him in our hearts as his commandment, is itself law. How different would the world look if it were marked by a "culture of love," in which "the desire for peace would bring an end to strife, pardon would overcome hatred, and revenge give way to forgiveness," as a prayer says.

"The one who loves another has fulfilled the law" (Rom 13:8) declares Paul succinctly. Such a person has a heart not of stone but of flesh, a gift of God's Spirit.

The love that is in our heart meets the other in just the way that person wants to be loved. It "bears all things, believes all things, hopes all things, endures all things" (1 Cor 13:7). Such love casts out fear and is not afraid to get hurt. It makes us free and happy. It is a foretaste of heaven, for "where love and goodness are, there is God."

2 Take the Bull by the Horns

The desert fathers of the first centuries of the Christian era, true masters in knowledge of the soul, constantly speak of the danger of acedia. They are referring to a lethargy and paralysis that affects our driving forces, a deep sadness, perhaps even a weariness and a disgust for life. Such an inner state can be a sign of depression, it can appear in the form of a life crisis, and it may even become firmly established as a fundamental attitude.

Besides these common and serious forms there is also a kind of everyday acedia. We're all familiar with a kind of "noonday devil" that comes over us for a short time. Who hasn't sometimes had, in the rush of day-to-day affairs, a sleepy and sluggish hour? And then there are the times when these hours become more frequent.

All this can have a physical cause. Maybe

I need to get a good night's sleep once again, maybe I need more exercise, maybe I even need a complete checkup.

Sometimes it also helps to simply take the bull by the horns, just tackle a job (possibly an unpleasant one) and shoulder it. Or I can give myself a kick and resume this or that contact, turning to others and getting involved in their worries and problems. Often enough, I realize later that in doing so I've completely forgotten my own inner pain. And the "demon" is banished!

3 What Remains

"**M**y vocation, at last I have found it…. My vocation is love!"

This cry comes from Thérèse of Lisieux. Photographs of this woman, who died more than a hundred years ago, show her mostly smiling, a sign that she was happy amid every challenge to her vocation, in her largely hidden life (she was only twenty-four years old when she died) behind the walls of the cloister.

"My vocation is love!" Isn't this true of every human being? We know that people wither away from lack of love, but where they find love they blossom. At some time or other every one of us has probably experienced that love makes us happy. "Also unhappy!" many would argue. That's true because love is very fragile, and if it fails we may carry the scars with us all our life. But it's also true that love is never in vain.

The only thing that remains at the end of my life is how much I've loved. The only thing that remains at the end of this day is how much I've loved today.

The Golden Rule

What gloomy scenario is delivered to our door every day through the news, and what negative things do we ourselves often experience in our job-related daily life: competition, harassment, domination, over-assertiveness…. At the same time, it would really be so easy:

"You shall love your neighbor
as yourself!"
(Lev 19:18; Lk 10:27)

This biblical maxim is found as the "golden rule" in all major religions, either in the negative form, "Do not do to others what you would not have them do to you!" or in the positive form used by Jesus:

"Do to others whatever you
would have them do to you!"
(Mt 7:12)

We immediately sense, "That's it!" It's actually so simple, almost self-evident. Yet it would be a revolution if people followed it. And how different the world would look if whole groups, indeed nations and countries, would make these words their own.

An illusion? Utopia? Let's go ahead and leave these questions unanswered. At any rate, it's a vision that's planted deep in the hearts of us humans. For all the pragmatists among us, the golden rule is still a principle that makes sense as a basis for the life of any form of community. Sense enough that for one whole day I'll take as my motto:

I will do to others whatever
I would have them do to me!

5 Advance Preparation

"Hello! We know each other, right? We've already met!" — "Where do you know me from?" — "I've been praying for you for a long time."

This happened once to the former Bishop of Aachen, Klaus Hemmerle.

A strange incident that has often crossed my mind ever since he told me about it. It reminds me of the importance of advance preparation. When I'm prepared for the other before an important meeting, when I've carried that person with me in my thoughts and even in my prayers, the meeting becomes different.

I try to go in with an open mind, with respect, and with that healthy sense of anticipation that is part of a conscious existence.

This way I don't just "tumble" into the conversation. Without adequate advance preparation, I risk running my counterpart over, being full of myself, perhaps even guided by strong concerns. As a result, I have no heart, no open ear for the other.

A real encounter is a miracle; a person who encounters me is a gift; that person's gifts enrich me. It depends on my advance preparation!

Do You Know What Hurts Me?

"**Y**ou say you love me. Do you know what hurts me?"

"No."

"Then you don't really love me!"

This Jewish wisdom saying brings home to us vividly and profoundly just how superficial many of our relationships are. Can we say of anyone that we already know what really hurts them? Who knows what hurts me? Among colleagues in the workplace, among people who share our leisure activities, even in our own family and among friends, we sometimes get the feeling that we really have nothing important to say to each other. Maybe we suspect that the other person really has much to say, but this isn't the place for it.

We discover the very opposite. Wherever someone, very discreetly, finds a way to talk about what hurts them, about their pain, their loneliness and their guilt, the conversation can take on a whole new depth. Pain can create an intense bond between people. When I know something about another person's pain, something of that person's mystery is given to me. When I allow someone to share in my pain, I reveal something of my own mystery.

It doesn't happen always and everywhere, because when we do this we make ourselves more vulnerable. That's the price of being able to really love and be loved! Yet I'm sure there are many opportunities to be more open and more mindful of what hurts another, and at the same time be more open to sharing what hurts *me*. Where that happens, we meet one another at a much deeper place.

7 Called by Name

If I'm addressed by name, I react differently than if someone wants something from me anonymously ("namelessly"). If I'm addressed by name, I'm being referred to in a more personal manner. I was no more responsible for giving myself a name than I was for giving myself life. The name makes it clear that I'm always more than what I am just by myself. The Bible tells us that God has called us by name and repeatedly calls us again when we hide from him. We are already shown this in the story of the garden of Paradise:

"Adam, where are you?" (Gen 3:9). "I have called you by name," says the Lord (Is 43:1). He has written me in the palm of his hand (see Is 49:16).

There could hardly be a more beautiful expression of how valuable and unique I am in God's eyes. This precisely is the expression of his creative love:

"I have loved you with
an everlasting love." (Jer 31:3)

These words (often I can hardly believe them) include me! And every person (often I can hardly believe that either)! They include those who cross my path today, those I know by name, along with the many nameless faces. These words apply to them all:

"I have loved you with
an everlasting love."

If I remind myself of this every once in a while I'll look at people differently. Even myself.

Seeking *God*

four

A Resounding Yes

There are situations in which we hit rock bottom. At best we would like to call it quits. It's over, hopeless. How good it is at such times to know that God never writes anyone off, that with God a new beginning is always possible.

The Lutheran theologian Paul Tillich says:

"Grace strikes us when we are in great pain and restlessness…. It strikes us when we feel that … we have violated another life…. It strikes us when our disgust for our own being … has become intolerable…. Sometimes at that moment a wave of light breaks into our darkness, and it is as though a voice were saying: 'You are accepted. You are accepted …' "[1]

To the question about God, to the question of whether he exists, what he is like,

---

1. Paul Tillich, *The Shaking of the Foundations* (Farmington Hills: Charles Scribner's Sons, 1955).

where he is in my life — to these questions there are many answers, none of them complete. We can never comprehend the mystery of God. Faith tells us that God is very near and yet transcendent, unfathomable mystery and at the same time like a father or mother. An incredible revelation, because it means that he himself is interested in us. He wants to find a way to us, and he will, as long as we don't consciously set up a roadblock. Perhaps just at a moment when we are "down," it is then that a voice seems to be saying: "You are accepted."

2 The Carpet

Have you ever looked at the underside of a carpet? You can't make out much of the rich colors and the beauty of the pattern. What you see there is gray and drab, along with many knots.

Might this not be an image of the "underside" of our life? Of the drabness of our daily life, of the half measures that often seem to make up our life, of the things patched up after a fashion, and of the insoluble problems that make life so difficult for us?

The idea that all this is supposed to produce a beautiful pattern on the upper side is not easy for us to accept.

To be sure, there are moments when we get a hint of it. Moments when we see in a flash of insight that life is not just a series of coincidences strung together, that it's more than the same homemade successes (and defeats). Moments when we get the impression that a hand is holding us, supporting us, leading us on. But is anyone weaving them into a beautiful carpet? The words of the apostle Paul make me quite hopeful in this regard:

> "We know that all things work together for good for those who love God." (Rom 8:28)

3 Within Ourselves or Nowhere

In Bertholt Brecht's *Galileo,* to the repeated question of where God is in his system, Galileo answers: "Within ourselves or nowhere."

God in us? Really? Then I ought to have found him long ago!

Aren't we running ahead of ourselves every day? Do we even have time for ourselves? Not to amuse ourselves yet again, but time for ourselves that is completely personal. In the words of Karl Valentin: "Today I'm going to pay a visit to myself to see whether or not I'm at home."

There where I'm completely by myself, where I put up with myself or am happy with myself, there it can happen that suddenly I'm no longer alone. I know that I have been spoken to by another. I sense his nearness. If God isn't within me, where else am I supposed to find him?

But perhaps I've also found God in another person when I myself felt very empty. "Within ourselves or nowhere." If I can't sense his presence in me, maybe in another?

Remain on the lookout for God as I try to be completely by myself. Remain on the lookout for God as I try to be completely with others. These are my two keynotes for today!

4 The Whole in a Fragment

Who doesn't dream of great success in their life? Yet what we hold in our hands is often just a fragment. Don't we sometimes get the feeling that real life has passed us by? That, day after day, our life has been the victim of superficiality and routine, of the drabness that hides the brightness we long to see there? Our life consists of an endless number of days, drab days, in which our happiness is hidden. Yet in the very midst of our routine, life wants to celebrate encounter. Reality, the people around me, various hardships, life just as it is, my life: all these are the things God uses to speak to me, to enter into relationship with me.

In the way I deal with reality, with the people around me, with various hardships, with life just as it is, with my life, I can respond to God, I can enter into a conversation with him, I can ask him again: What do you want me to do now, God?

Everything can become part of this conversation. When this happens, color comes into our life. What seems fragmentary, an insignificant tiny piece, has entered into relationship with that which embraces everything and could give our life breadth — always. On January 6, 1945, a few weeks before his death, the Jesuit Alfred Delp wrote: "We must set sail in a never-ending wind; only then will we see what journey we are capable of. A free and unconditional encounter with the Lord God gives us our own space.... A bended knee and empty hands held out are both essential gestures of a free human being.... Hand yourself over to your God and you will again possess yourself."

Seeking and Finding God in All Things

A God-seeker came to the rabbi and said to him: "I'll give you a kopeck if you can tell me where God lives!"

The rabbi answered him: "And I'll give you a hundred kopecks if you can tell me where God doesn't live."

I see what I carry in my heart.

When I'm happy, I find the thing that produces happiness in my surroundings and among my fellow human beings.

When I'm sad, the whole world often seems sad to me.

When I carry God in my heart, I also find him between the lines of my everyday life. It is essential, as Ignatius of Loyola aptly said, to seek and find God in all things.

How? I'd like to say that for happiness there's no recipe. It would rob these words of their mysteriousness and fascination. Certainly it's not a matter of desperately seeking God "behind" things. We wouldn't be taking his creation very truly or very seriously. And we wouldn't find him *in* all things.

How do we seek and find God in all things? Two words, which still preserve the mystery, can provide a clue: wonder and gratitude.

6 God Is Always Other

God Is Other was the German title of the 1968 bestseller, *Honest to God,* from the pen of Anglican bishop John A. T. Robinson. At the time, the book eliminated many all too human ideas of God and expectations of him. It upset many people, including me. Since then I've learned that I must constantly examine my images of God. And when one of my familiar images shatters, I can watch a new and more accurate image appear.

The Jewish prohibition against making any image of God has a deep meaning. I cannot make for myself any image, according to my dimensions, of the great mystery we call God. If I do, it is no image of God.

Yet the Bible itself speaks of him in images: the image of a father and of one who is like a mother, of a shepherd and king, of a friend and lover. Such images can help us approach God, as long as in doing this we do not forget what Martin Buber says: "All ideas of God are just directional arrows or necessary thresholds that humans use on the path to God. But at the same time we must constantly transcend them and leave them behind. Humans do not experience the reality of God in these images and words, but only in a living encounter."

The thought that a living God desires to accompany me — us — throughout this day is enough to make my head spin.

7 Everything Begins with Desire

"Everything begins with desire," I read in Nelly Sachs. Do I still know what desire means? What *do* I desire? Today, this morning? Maybe a desire for quiet and relaxation, for a vacation or for more activity in my life, for change, for something thrilling and exciting, for something completely different?

Great! It means that desire is still alive, not extinguished under the ashes of dashed hopes, under the resigned realization that "things won't change any more; my life holds no promise."

As long as I still feel unrest, homesickness or wanderlust, a desire to be home more or to have more freedom, there is hope.

Let's follow this desire. The trail leads beyond to something greater than us, to something that, paradoxically, allows us to be fuller and more complete human beings. We are restless creatures with endless desires.

"Our heart is restless until it rests in you," wrote Augustine; in you who are perhaps unknown, who are greater, who are the God that lovingly embraces us.

Also available in the same series:

Mary
Four Weeks with the Mother of Jesus

Edited by Wolfang Bader and Stephen Liesenfeld

72 pages
ISBN: 978-1-56548-281-6

Pathways to God
Four Weeks on Faith, Hope and Charity

Robert F. Morneau

72 pages
ISBN: 978-1-56548-286-9

In preparation:

Fostering True Peace of Heart
Marc Foley

To order call 1-800-462-5980
or e-mail orders@newcitypress.com